ONLINE JOURNALISTS

BY JILL KEPPELER

Gareth Stevens
PUBLISHING

Please visit our website, www.garethstevens.com. For a free color catalog of all our high-quality books, call toll free 1-800-542-2595 or fax 1-877-542-2596.

Cataloging-in-Publication Data

Names: Keppeler, Jill.
Title: Online journalists / Jill Keppeler.
Description: New York : Gareth Stevens Publishing, 2020. | Series: Digital insiders | Includes glossary and index.
Identifiers: ISBN 9781538247556 (pbk.) | ISBN 9781538247570 (library bound) | ISBN 9781538247563 (6 pack)
Subjects: LCSH: Online journalism–Juvenile literature.
Classification: LCC PN4784.O62 K47 2020 | DDC 808′.06607–dc23

First Edition

Published in 2020 by
Gareth Stevens Publishing
111 East 14th Street, Suite 349
New York, NY 10003

Designer: Sarah Liddell
Editor: Lynn Moon

Photo credits: Cover, p. 1 Akkalak Aiempradit/Shutterstock.com; background texture used throughout VLADGRIN/ Shutterstock.com; screen texture used throughout majcot/Shutterstock.com; p. 5 Steve Cukrov/Shutterstock.com; p. 7 Alena Ozerova/Shutterstock.com; p. 9 Kaspars Grinvalds/Shutterstock.com; p. 11 Robert Giroux/Stringer/ Getty Images News/Getty Images; p. 13 (top) Casimiro PT/Shutterstock.com; p. 13 (bottom) AlexGrec/ Shutterstock.com; p. 15 Ben Gabbe/Stringer/Getty Images Entertainment/Getty Images; p. 17 (top) a katz/ Shutterstock.com; p. 17 (bottom) LightField Studios/Shutterstock.com; pp. 19, 21 GaudiLab/Shutterstock.com; p. 23 Africa Studio/Shutterstock.com; p. 25 (top) Hadrian/Shutterstock.com; p. 25 (bottom) leonrwoods/ Shutterstock.com; p. 29 Marco Foresti/Shutterstock.com.

Printed in the United States of America

Some of the images in this book illustrate individuals who are models. The depictions do not imply actual situations or events.

CPSIA compliance information: Batch #CW20GS: For further information contact Gareth Stevens, New York, New York at 1-800-542-2595.

CONTENTS

Words in the glossary appear in **bold** type the first time they are used in the text.

WHAT'S A JOURNALIST?

Where do you hear, see, or read news? Perhaps you hear things from your friends or see headlines in newspapers in the library. You probably also see news online. Many websites post news stories, and people then share them on **social media**. Online news can spread very quickly!

Journalists are people who work with the collecting, writing, and editing of news stories for newspapers, magazines, websites, television, or radio. Many journalists work for bigger organizations, but some don't. In the age of online journalism, all you really need is an internet connection, some skills, and a nose for news!

🔍 ON THE RISE

In 2018, at least nine in ten adults in the United States reported getting at least some of their news online. Also, people today are more likely to pick up their mobile device, such as a smartphone, to look for news instead of going to a computer.

THE POPULAR OLD IMAGE OF A JOURNALIST OFTEN SHOWS SOMEONE WRITING A STORY ON A TYPEWRITER. TODAY, JOURNALISTS ARE FAR MORE LIKELY TO BE TYPING ON A LAPTOP—OR EVEN ON THEIR PHONE!

NEWS ONLINE

You can find online news in many different forms. Sometimes, journalists post stories or videos on websites. Some journalists create **blogs** or **podcasts**. News apps and email newsletters also report headlines and stories. Other websites collect headlines from other sources and share them. And social media makes sharing the news even easier!

Online news sources often use many forms of social media to get their stories out there. Almost all news sites have pages on Facebook and accounts on Twitter. Many also use YouTube and Instagram. This makes it very simple to share news—but hard to control it once a story is out there.

SOCIAL MEDIA

Most types of social media only allow users over a certain age. You have to be at least 13 years old to have an account on Facebook, Twitter, YouTube, Instagram, Tumblr, Snapchat, or Pinterest. People under 13 can watch YouTube videos, but they can't have their own account. People under 18 also can't watch certain videos on YouTube.

THERE ARE WEBSITES AND APPS THAT MAKE NEWS FOR KIDS. IF YOU'RE INTERESTED, ASK A PARENT OR TRUSTED ADULT TO HELP YOU FIND THEM.

PRINT TO DIGITAL

Often, online journalists work for news organizations that also publish news in print or have a TV **broadcast**. Almost all newspapers or TV stations (also called **legacy** news outlets) have a website or social media accounts on which to post stories, videos, or other items. In a way, all journalists today are online journalists to some measure!

Legacy news outlets may only post some of their stories online, or only parts of each story. Their websites and social media accounts may also have facts that don't appear in their print products or broadcasts. The key is to make people want to see everything the news organization puts out.

🔍 GOING ONLINE

The first online news service started in 1980. The Associated Press and CompuServe internet service started making some newspaper content available online. Users paid a fee of $5 an hour for the text, or words, alone. It took a full minute for them to get 300 words of a story on their computer!

PARTS OF A NEWS WEBSITE

LIST OF DEPARTMENTS

MASTHEAD AT THE TOP

MAIN ART

HEADLINES

BYLINES

NEWSPAPER WEBSITES OFTEN HAVE LAYOUTS, OR ARRANGEMENTS, AND FEATURES THAT ARE SIMILAR TO THOSE OF PRINT NEWSPAPERS.

ONLINE ONLY

Some news sources started online as websites, apps, or social media. Popular online-born news sources include the **technology** website CNET and the business news site Business Insider. Others include Slate, TMZ, Deadspin, and Bleacher Report.

Many online-born news sources are not as trusted as legacy sources. In 2018, Simmons **Research** revealed a list of 38 news sources ranked by how much Americans trust them. The top ten most-trusted sources were legacy news sources. The six least-trusted were online-only news sources. However, even the most-trusted news source, the *Wall Street Journal*, was only trusted by about 58 percent of Americans.

AT THE BOTTOM

The less-trusted news websites tend to be partisan sources. "Partisan" means strongly supporting a certain cause, group, or leader. Partisan news sources often write stories that support one political group, or put down other political groups. These sources are not as trustworthy because journalists are supposed to stick to facts and keep their reporting balanced.

THE *SEATTLE POST-INTELLIGENCER* WAS A PRINT NEWSPAPER FOR 146 YEARS, BUT IN 2009 IT WENT FULLY ONLINE IN ORDER TO STAY IN BUSINESS.

NOSE FOR NEWS

Are you interested in being an online journalist? While you can study journalism in college, you also can start learning about it now. To be an online journalist, you need to have a way to get your stories out there. But first, you need stories!

A good news story tells people something they didn't know before. It might be something they need to know. It also might be something that's less important, but very interesting. Keep your eyes open. Many journalists always keep a camera, a notepad, and pen on them, just in case they see something they might want to write about.

🔍 LEARN FROM PROS

One good way to learn about journalism is to watch and read the news! See what respected journalists do and how they handle stories. Learn how to write well and practice **interviewing** people you know. Reading trusted newspapers like the *Wall Street Journal* also can help you become a better writer.

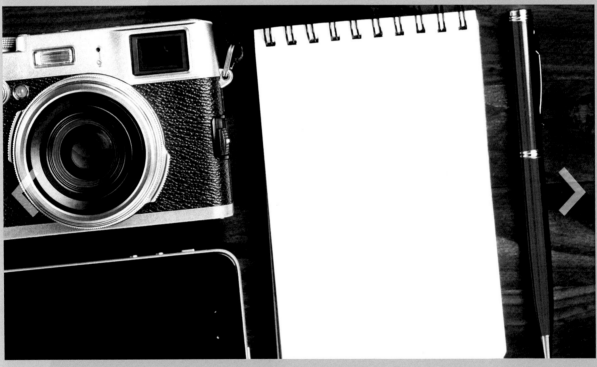

IN A 2018 SIMMONS RESEARCH STUDY, THE *WALL STREET JOURNAL* WAS THE ONLY NEWSPAPER IN THE TOP FIVE MOST-TRUSTED NEWS SOURCES IN THE UNITED STATES. IT ALSO HAS A WEBSITE.

One way to learn about journalism is to join your school newspaper. If your school doesn't have one, maybe you can start one! Some school newspapers are online only, some are print only, and some have both online and print papers. There are ways to easily and cheaply create websites. Ask a teacher to help create a newspaper staff and website. Or, your school's website director might be able to add the newspaper to the school website.

If you have a local newspaper, you could also check to see if they accept articles from young writers.

🔍 KID REPORTERS

Some big national news sources, such as *Sports Illustrated Kids* and *Time for Kids* magazine, accept kid reporters for their websites. Scholastic News even has a Kids Press Corps. Check out their websites to read their news stories and learn more about how to become a kid reporter.

SCHOLASTIC KID REPORTER MAXWELL SUPRENANT, SHOWN, INTERVIEWS THE AUTHOR OF CAPTAIN UNDERPANTS, DAV PILKEY, IN 2017.

INTERVIEWING

Interviewing is a very important skill for any journalist, no matter their age. It's not just as simple as asking questions. Before interviewing someone, it's important to research the person and the subject you'll be interviewing them about. That way, you don't have to waste time getting background when the interview starts. Write down a list of questions you want to ask.

Even if you record an interview in **audio** or video, take notes too. Sometimes technology fails! Notes are also good to help you remember the setting. Be on time and be polite to the person you're interviewing. Make eye contact and speak clearly.

YOUTUBE AND YOU

Even if you are under 13, you can ask a parent or trusted adult to help you start a YouTube channel on their account. It's a great way to start learning behind-the-scenes skills, like recording and editing sound and video. The adult should OK each video before you post it.

SOMETIMES REPORTING THE NEWS IS A TEAM
EFFORT, ESPECIALLY IF YOU WANT TO START FILMING
OR RECORDING AUDIO OF YOUR STORIES. FIND FRIENDS
TO HELP YOU REPORT THE LATEST SCOOP!

TOOLS AND TIPS

Journalists don't just use the internet and social media to get their stories out there. Today, they often use these tools to find information as well. People put a lot of information on the internet, and journalists can use many tools to find that information. This could range from things as simple as acquiring someone's phone number to discovering that someone lied about an important event.

Search engines, such as Google, offer ways to hunt for information. Social media **profiles** and posts can show what people think. However, a good reporter is **skeptical**. Even if you see information online, you have to make sure it's true!

GOOD SEARCHING

The first rule of good internet searching is to be exact. This means to clearly state what you're looking for. Use quotation marks around words to find those specific words. Use "OR" between words to look for two terms at once. Make sure you look for good sources!

OFFICIAL WEBSITES FOR SCHOOLS, GOVERNMENT ORGANIZATIONS, OR OTHER GROUPS OFTEN HAVE **RELIABLE** INFORMATION. THIS CAN BE A GOOD PLACE TO START YOUR RESEARCH.

GOOD SOURCES

A news story is only as good as its sources. For example, let's say that you heard a story at school that a popular teacher is leaving. If you wrote a news story using only rumors, or information that's not proven to be true, you'd look pretty silly if the news turned out to be fake! The teacher might be mad at you too. You could get in trouble if your fake story caused problems.

In this case, the first thing you should do is ask the teacher if they are leaving. Unless you have proof, you don't have a story!

🔍 WHO'S ANONYMOUS?

Sometimes, news sources use anonymous sources. This means the source isn't named in the story, though the journalist knows who it is. That might be because the source is worried about getting in trouble. Journalists need to be very careful about using anonymous sources. Many news outlets don't use them at all.

IF YOU FEEL LIKE YOU CAN'T TRUST A STORY, LOOK TO SEE IF ANY OTHER NEWS SOURCES ARE REPORTING IT. IF THEY ARE, ARE THEY REPORTING IT THE SAME WAY?

TRUST AND ETHICS

Many news sources have codes of ethics. These are sets of rules based on what's right and what's wrong. The Society of **Professional** Journalists (SPJ) also has a code of ethics. It includes rules such as always telling the truth, being fair, and never taking money or gifts to tell a story a certain way. A news outlet that has an ethics code and sticks to it is more likely to be trustworthy.

The SPJ code also includes labeling opinion pieces clearly as opinion. People in a news story may state opinions when they're interviewed, but the journalist should not.

FACT VS. OPINION

Opinion pieces in a news source may be called commentary, editorials, op-eds, or columns. They're often in a part of a website or newspaper just for them. They should have the writer's name and title clearly stated. Most people like reading opinions that agree with their own. Sometimes, though, it's good to read different ones.

YOU MAY NOT BE A PROFESSIONAL JOURNALIST, BUT EVEN IF YOU'RE A STUDENT JOURNALIST, IT'S IMPORTANT TO STICK TO BASIC ETHICS. BAD JOURNALISM CAN HURT PEOPLE!

CHANGES AND CHALLENGES

Online journalism has changed the field of journalism in many ways. Many of these ways can be real challenges, or problems to overcome, for journalists and those looking for trustworthy news. News online can be updated and changed far more quickly than print or TV news. As news outlets try to get "scoops," or report on stories first, they might get things wrong in the rush to put news online.

Viral news, which is news that spreads very quickly through the internet, can also be a problem. Just because it spreads quickly doesn't mean it's true. In fact, often it's not!

HOW TO MAKE MONEY

One way online journalists can make money is by starting their own news websites. Then companies can pay to **advertise**, or make the public aware of, products or services on this website. The more visitors or traffic a website has, the more companies are often willing to pay for ads.

"CLICKBAIT" IS ONLINE CONTENT MADE TO ENCOURAGE PEOPLE TO CLICK ON A LINK TO ANOTHER WEBSITE. CLICKBAIT USES ATTENTION-GRABBING HEADLINES THAT AREN'T ALWAYS TRUE.

Today, so many people get their news online that many print newspapers are closing. Hundreds of newspapers have stopped printing in the past 15 years or so. As people stopped buying and reading print newspapers, businesses stopped advertising in them. Newspapers stopped making money and more closed. However, people still want news. Who will step up to report it? Online journalists!

With the rise of clickbait and fake news sites, knowing how to find and tell the truth will be a good skill to have. Do you have what it takes?

🔍 FAKE OR REAL?

Fake news has become popular for some writers because they can make lots of money writing it. The more clicks a story gets, the more they make. Remember, though, that sometimes people call news "fake" even if it's real, just because they don't like it.

SIGNS OF FAKE NEWS

MANY SPELLING MISTAKES OR USE OF ALL CAPITAL LETTERS

NO WRITER'S NAME ON THE ARTICLE

NO CONTACT INFORMATION OR CODE OF ETHICS FOR THE NEWS OUTLET

SHOCKING OR ATTENTION-GRABBING HEADLINE

HEADLINE DOES NOT MATCH THE CONTENT

CONTENT TRIES TO MAKE THE READER MAD OR UPSET

THE NEWS IS OLD OR REPORTS ON SOMETHING THAT'S SUPPOSED TO HAPPEN IN THE FUTURE

THERE ARE NO OR FEW QUOTES, OR STATEMENTS, FROM REAL PEOPLE

THERE'S LOTS OF OPINION IN THE STORY BUT IT'S NOT LABELED AS OPINION IN SOME WAY

USE YOUR NOSE FOR NEWS TO SNIFF OUT THE BAD STUFF! THESE SIGNS OF FAKE NEWS WILL HELP YOU TELL IF A NEWS SOURCE IS NOT TRUSTWORTHY.

LISTEN, LEARN, AND REPORT!

Journalism will look different in the years to come, but there will always be a need for people to report the truth. How can you become one of them? You can practice the basic skills right now. Learn how to tell real news from fake news, practice interviewing people, learn computer skills, read a lot, and write, write, write!

With a teacher or parent's help, you might be able to become a student journalist and share your writing online. When you're old enough, learn how to use social media. Watch and read pieces by trusted journalists. Someday, you can be one of them!

JOURNALISTS IN HISTORY

Journalists have made a big difference in US history. Letters printed in early newspapers encouraged people to speak out about the British before the American Revolution. Many journalists and newspapers called for an end to slavery in the 1800s. In 1974, President Richard Nixon left office in part because of a newspaper's reporting. What's next?

TAKING PICTURES, FILMING AND EDITING VIDEOS, AND RECORDING AND EDITING AUDIO ARE ALL USEFUL SKILLS FOR AN ONLINE JOURNALIST. YOU CAN START LEARNING THESE SKILLS NOW!

GLOSSARY

advertise: online, printed, or broadcast pieces that are meant to sell something or make an announcement.

audio: sound heard on a recording or broadcast

blog: a website on which someone writes about what they think and do

broadcast: a radio or TV program. Also, to send out by radio or TV.

interview: to talk to someone to get information for something. Also, a meeting between a reporter and another person to get information for a news story.

legacy: in media, forms of mass communication that existed before the internet, such as newspapers

podcast: a program like a radio or TV show, but downloaded, or copied, from the internet

professional: having to do with a job someone does for a living

profile: information and settings of a certain internet user on a certain website or app

reliable: able to be trusted or believed

research: to study something carefully or collect information on it. Also, careful information gathering that is done to find and report new knowledge about something.

skeptical: having doubts about something

social media: ways to communicate online using websites or smartphone applications, or apps, through which people create online communities to share information, ideas, personal messages, and more

technology: the way people do something using tools and the tools that they use. Also, the practical application of specialized knowledge.

FOR MORE INFORMATION

BOOKS

Dell, Pamela. *Understanding the News*. North Mankato, MN: Capstone Press, 2019.

Fromm, Megan. *Gathering and Sharing Digital Information*. New York, NY: Rosen Publishing's Rosen Central, 2015.

Lane, Paul. *Viral News on Social Media*. New York, NY: PowerKids Press, 2019.

WEBSITES

Get Smart About News
newslit.org/get-smart/
Find activities, quizzes, and graphics about news literacy on this website by the News Literacy Project.

Scholastic News Kids Press Corps
kpcnotebook.scholastic.com
Read articles written by kid reporters and learn more about how to join the Kids Press Corps.

YouTube Teen Kids News
www.youtube.com/channel/UC5btLwBEeYNdYc56YZyBjzw
Watch news segments designed for and reported by young journalists.

INDEX